HummingBirds

BOOK 2 of 3

Coloring Book

Mother Nature Series

Author Artist   Jeri Lee C.Ht.

ISBN: 9798385871506

This BOOK
BELONGS TO

____

Name

____

Date

Hummingbirds

Hummingbirds are the smallest bird species in the world, weighing between 2-20 grams. They have long wings that can beat up to 80 times per second! Hummingbirds feed by hovering in front of flowers and sipping nectar through their long beaks. . These tiny birds can fly up to 60 miles per hour during migration season. Hummingbirds can also fly backward and hover in midair for several seconds at a time – an amazing feat! Unlike other birds, hummingbirds don't rely on walking or hopping; instead, they use their feet only for perching or clinging onto branches while sleeping and resting.. The average lifespan of a hummingbird is 3-5 years, but some species can live as long as ten years in captivity Hummingbirds come in a variety of colors, ranging from iridescent blues and greens to browns and even black. The most common coloration is green with red or orange spots on the throat. Males tend to have brighter plumage than females, which helps them stand out during courtship displays. Mating habits vary between species but generally involve elaborate aerial displays involving dives, U-turns, hovering, and chases. Males also produce loud vocalizations that can be heard up to several hundred meters away as part of their courtship behavior. Once these displays have attracted a female, she usually chooses one male for mating purposes; if multiple males are present, the strongest displayer is generally selected.

Mother Earth Series

Welcome to my Mother Earth Series of Coloring Books! This series was created to inspire respect for our planet and its many families of life. It focuses on the beauty, harmony, and balance of nature that is so essential to sustaining life on earth. Through these books, we hope to bring awareness of how important it is for us all to work together in protecting our environment and creating a better future for generations to come. The Mother Earth series explores the delicate relationship between humans and nature by featuring stunning artwork depicting The birds, Bees, Butterflies and plants. Animals, both on land and at sea I feature in my series Save the Planet. Please check them out and more. Each page encourages interaction with vibrant colors while providing an opportunity for reflection on our impact upon this beautiful world we call home. The message behind each book is simple: Respect Nature! We can make a difference in preserving our planet if we choose eco-friendly solutions when possible such as using reusable items instead of disposable ones; conserving energy through efficient lighting; eating organic food grown without harmful chemicals; reducing water waste; recycling materials whenever possible; supporting renewable energy sources like solar or wind power; avoiding single-use plastics whenever you can — just some examples from what could be done every day in order to protect our environment. We are living beings within a complex web of interconnectedness that includes plants, animals (including ourselves), air quality, water resources – even climate change -all intricately linked together. We owe it not only ourselves but also future generations who will inherit this magnificent world that has been entrusted into our care today—to recognize its importance and use wisdom when choosing actions which affect the environment around us now & forevermore! Thank you for joining us as part of this journey towards a sustainable future – one coloring book at a time! If you enjoy my work, plesase leave me a positive review.

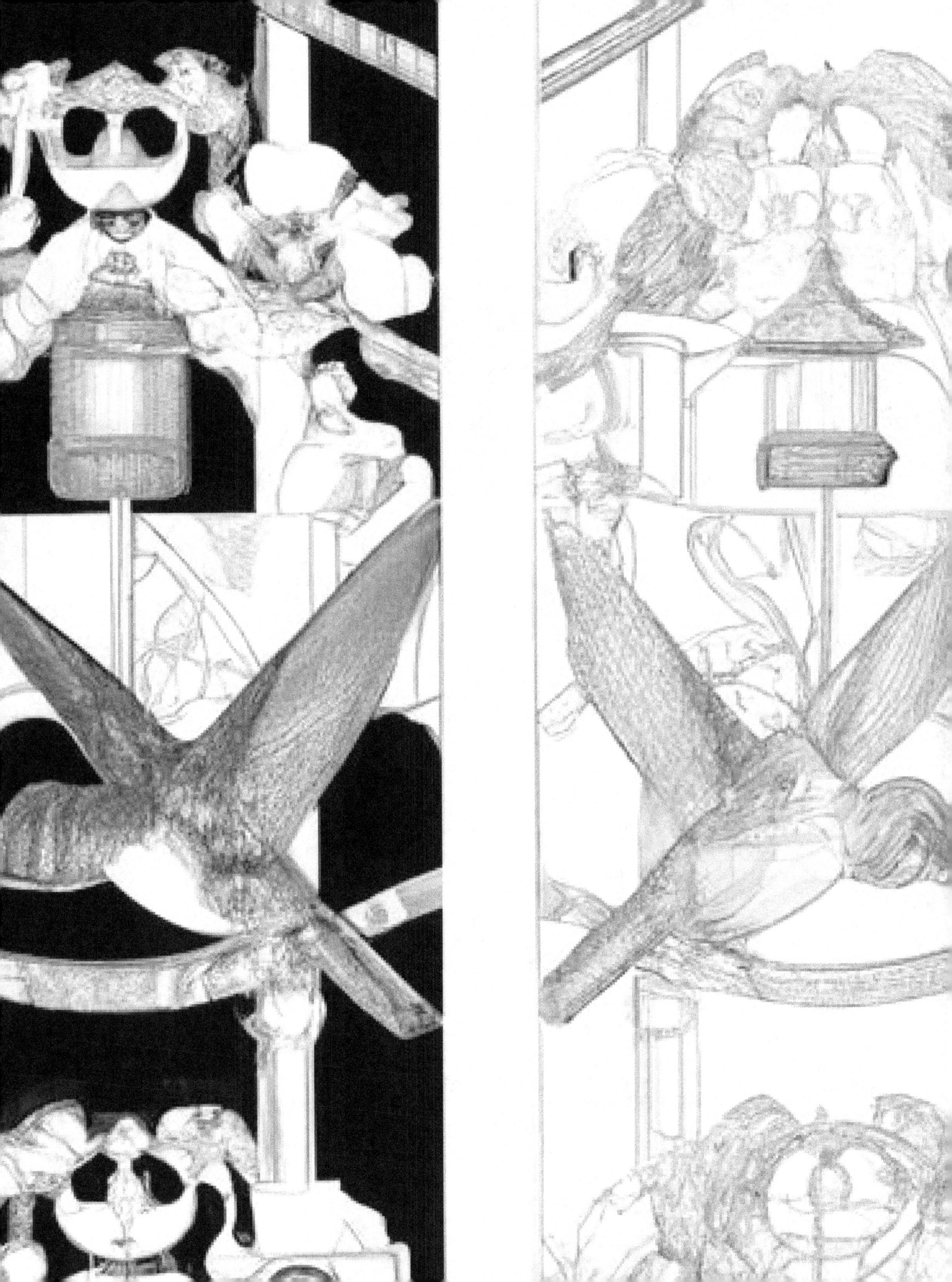

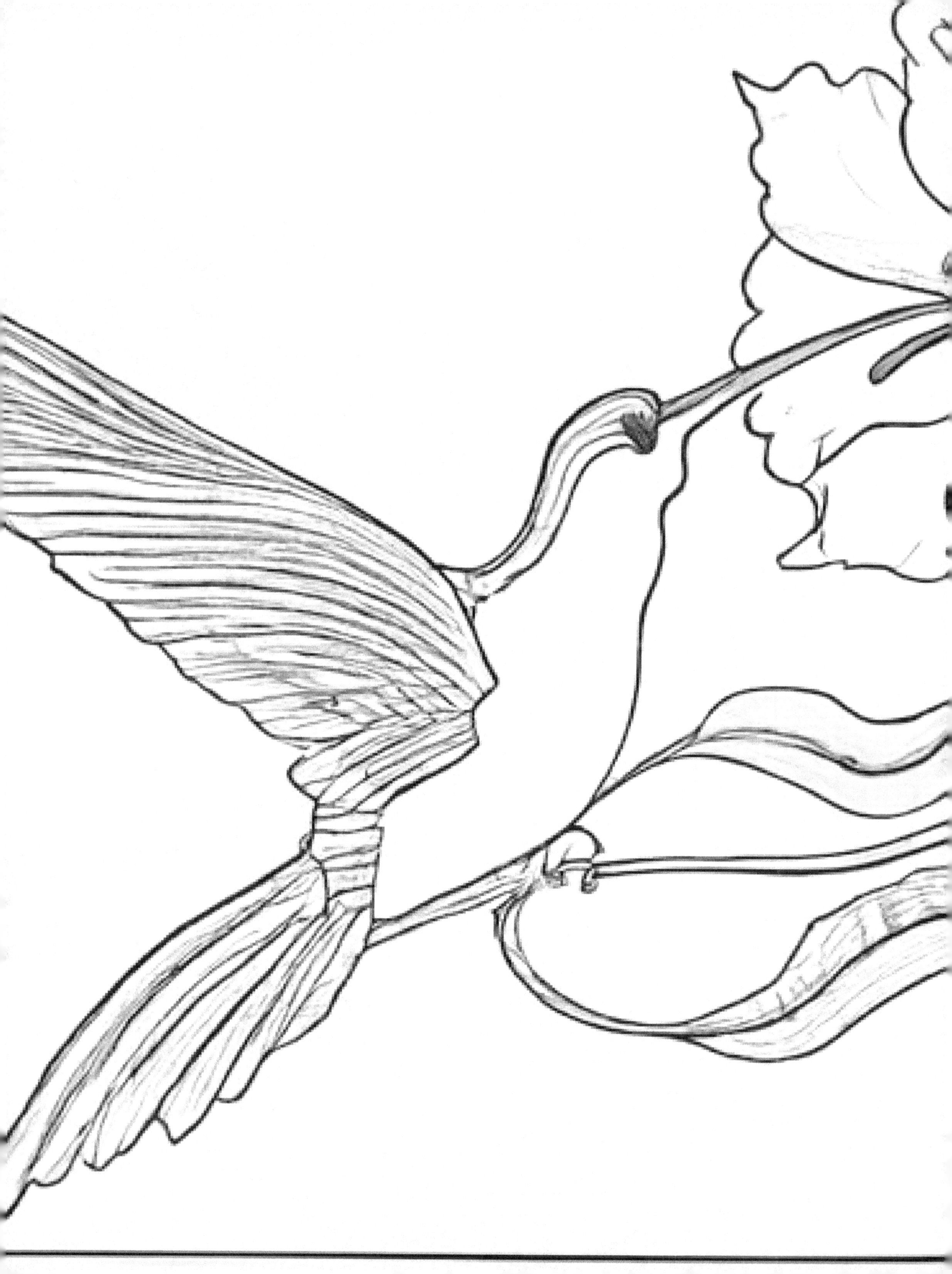

Thank You For Purchasing my Book

If you enjoyed it

Please give me a good review

You might also enjoy my other coloring book Series

Save the Planet Series
If you enjoy my books please give me a Positive review.

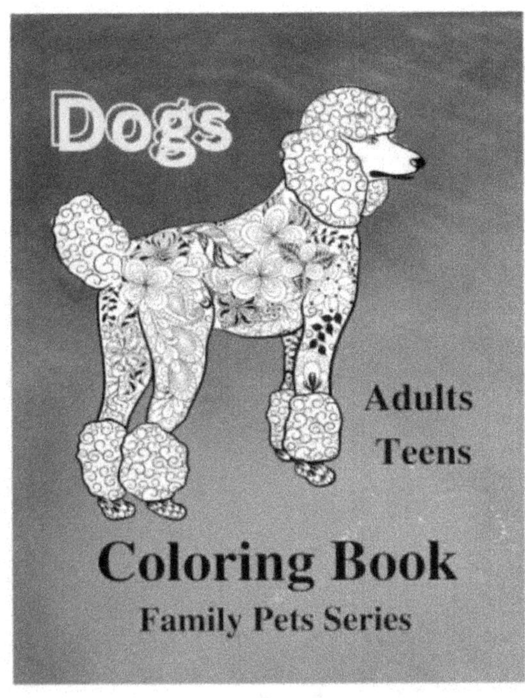

Many MORE

More Pet Books you might Enjoy

UNIVERSAL

PEACE